ANY PARTICULAR DAY

ANY PARTICULAR DAY

Nadine Brummer

Shoestring Press

Printed by imprintdigital
Upton Pyne, Exeter
www.imprintdigital.net

Typeset by types of light
typesoflight@gmail.com

Published by Shoestring Press
19 Devonshire Avenue, Beeston, Nottingham, NG9 1BS
(0115) 925 1827
www.shoestringpress.co.uk

First published 2013

Cover painting © Margaret Richards

ISBN 978-1-907356-66-7

ACKNOWLEDGEMENTS

Some of these poems were first published in the chapbook *Spectres* (Eyelet Books, 2008).

Acknowledgements are also due to the editors of *Artemis, Staple, The Dark Horse* and *The Interpreter's House*.

The opening image of 'Valentine' derives from a painting by Marie-Louise von Motesiczky.

I am warmly appreciative of Ruth Sharman's sustained and sustaining interest and helpful feed-back.

As always, I am especially grateful to my editor and publisher, John Lucas, for his punctilious comments, suggestions and unfailing support.

CONTENTS

Nanotechnology and the Fungus Gnat   3
Trout   4
And, Yes, One is Moved by Legs   6
Mantra   8
Almost Seeing   9
The Look of Apples   10
Talking to Myself when Sane   11
A Dream of Gardens   12
Windfalls   14
Sunflowers   16
Two Cut Sunflowers   17
Aquilegias   18
On an Island   20
Citadel on Kefalonia   21
"And the gulls are there"   22
Valentine   24
Rose Bay Willow Herb   25
Doppelgänger   27
Henry Moore at Kew   28
Epithalamium in February   31
Blue   33
Red, Magenta, Gold   34
Spectres   36
Anyone Out There?   37
Full Moon and Owls   39
Magpie on Snow   40
Woodpigeons   42
What a Fisherman Told Me   43
The Steps of Horses   44
Hôtel San Rémy   45
Towards a Self-Portrait   46

Before the Storm   47
Venice, This Time   48
Mirrors   50
The Man in Fancy Dress   51
The Cave   53
On Edge   54
'Naked Portrait' – Lucian Freud   55
Working it Out   56
The Desire for Angels   57
Seconds   59
Statues   60
The Unknown Knight of Netherbury   62
The Emperor of Exmoor   63

For Margaret

Sometimes the visionary aspect of any particular day comes to your memory of it and it opens to you over time.

—Marilynne Robinson, *Gilead*

NANOTECHNOLOGY AND THE FUNGUS GNAT

For the first time made visible,
fungus-gnats on the roof of a cave
remote as myth. And, yes, Arachne
came to mind the night we viewed
those mites, and their downhang
of shining. Heads were spinning
thread after thread while abdomens
delivered a white day-glo in the dark.
We saw the gorgeous structure of a trap
moths are drawn to, a veil of lights.

We can see anything we have a mind to.
Do moth-eyes see the beauty of the kill?
Are they equipped for that transforming vision
which shifts in tiny valves give rise to?
I like to think that different kinds of death
are possible, that bioluminescence grants
"the brightness of the spirit of the Lord",
at least, a consciousness of ravishment,
to creatures that can't help themselves,
helpless for light.

TROUT

If I'd Chardin's skill
to make a still-life
from life still there,
the ebb and flow
of this trout's colour,
rose and silvergilt,
the moiled black
of patches shaped like gills
with all the breathing power
black has when luminous;
if I could catch,
painterly, that spurt
of red on knifepoint
dug into the throat
unzipping pulp and slub
when I'm unsure
of spleen or gut, or what
the size and scope
of fish-brain is;
if I could get to grips
with the slipperiness
of answers to the question
"Did it hurt – head
dashed against a stone
and that last gulp?" –
I think I'd focus
on that still expressive
eye, to show
no look of horror

but the brilliance
of a mirror where
reflections go
into a room that grows
as you approach the glass.

AND, YES, ONE IS MOVED BY LEGS

Legs kept on going round
and round, mechanical
as well-wound clockwork
struggling, it seemed, to right
bodies anyhow heaped
in a mass, glass grave.
Nose pressed to a restaurant's
window-tank I stared
at Gargantuan crabs
not seeing straight,
myself I mean, remembering
Long Mile beach, Tofino
and half an inch of shell
scuttling on sand.

I'd knelt to inspect
legs daintily hinged, thighs
spotted like fishnet tights –
not that one could sex
a crab patterned on that scale
or work out its lifestyle –
Did the reek of kelp
blown in its squidgy face
propel that mite's gait?
Could it hear itself
creak, or the crack
of moonsnail eggs hatching
into movements too small
to keep up with oceans?
Was his/her life shaped

to cope with a tide
running out, a creature
not big enough to eat
like those giants
I saw in Seattle
walking away from being dead?

MANTRA

For years I've said those words
to myself as a mantra
when wanting something
that always eludes
then today I stroked the cat on my lap
and seeing the glint of gold hairs
here and there, an irregular pattern
in dark, brown fur outshining
a lamp's electric yellow
in a dynamic of light
beyond nerves and brain,
seeing that gleam and sensing
a pulse of extra life
right through me
as if fingers touched static
I was stilled, not needing
the far, the high, the wild
only this moment of domestic
vision, remembering
a library room
and Peter Matthiessen's
reply to my question
would he go back
to the Himalayas
to track the animal
he'd failed to find
"When you are ready
the snow-leopard appears."

ALMOST SEEING

On frosty days I go upstairs
for a view of a row of trees on a hill
receiving the last of the sun.

Branches and twigs are now a frame
for stained glass, the way they take on
first apple-green and then that flush

redgold, flame, fire, ember
colours that change their pitch
before pitch comes. How many reds

does black require? The winter sky's
not firm or molten but in-between
like brushwork on canvas:

sunset ends in a deepening glow
a nearly phosphorescent white
and then the trees' impasto blackness,

that drama of their seeming more alive
powered by light that's gone
and night to come

as if black is where light's action is.
And having seen with my own eyes
the letting-go of sunset done by trees

I come to Rothko's layered reds
and late Black Forms
almost to where the sunset goes.

THE LOOK OF APPLES

Why, he asked, did I want
to write about apples;
had I anything new to say?
Hadn't I read Frost's
'After Apple Picking'?
Hadn't I seen enough? –
Palmer's dreamt-up tree
bowed down with the weight
of crimson and Cézanne's
fruit of the earth made flesh
on his kitchen table,
the word of the tree made flesh
in one haptic moment.

"Tell me," I said,
"how I came to this place
where each year I see,
level with my eye
from my bedroom window
this one tree, in autumn,
packed with solid glow
as if the sun had found
a new angle on fruit
too small, too hard, too sour
even for birds to peck,
as if light shows how red
compacted into globes
may be continuous with love
where looking satisfies
more than eating does."

TALKING TO MYSELF WHEN SANE

The white magnolia is out –
say nothing, words interrupt
sensation, say nothing of
the Bride of Christ once seen
in your own head, a dazzling
one-off hallucination
that came between inside and out:
or say a treehead pours its light
in buds opening up
as chalices – the self
when hollow like a cup
may be too fragile
to contain perception
unless it breaks.

A DREAM OF GARDENS

Those lidded pots, storage-jars
of seeds inside the heads
of oriental poppies aren't
pythoi in the ruins of Knossos
a garden's not a royal palace
but mind works wonders with
the craft of plants' diverse
reproductive powers – green
pods, ovaries that house
barely visible eggs –
mind wonders how
from specks and nubs
from nothing much underground
orange-red explodes
and there's that surge
of urgent blue we call
Johnson's Blue geranium
as if we knew
the real names of flowers
or colours wrapped in light
like the Hebrews' name
for God, ineffable.

And mind – does it exist
apart from brain and nerves?
Perhaps it is
the Higgs boson of the body
making heads into big
storage-jars of seminal
ideas that infloresce

when we perceive
what it is we see –
calyx, tendril, tree,
examined anatomies
of axons, dendrites, fruitfly
ovaries under a microscope
those little candelabra
which may illuminate
fertility in women
but not the mind's
own conceptions –
its dream of gardens.

WINDFALLS

How do you measure the size
of a sound that exceeds
its noise? It's as if
apples dropping knock
on earth's door, not
that earth has a door
but something new breaks
through barrier of wall and gate
into a sunlit garden
with each small detonation,
the rhythm of a clock
gone wrong, telling the time
with start and stop
the way the heart does
in the silence after bad news.

Two friends died this year
prematurely, others fell sick.
And now apples that packed
two trees are mostly picked
and laid down, newspaper-wrapped –
drought, wars, tsunamis
all scrunched
round the firm bodies of fruit
in an exceptional September.

A half-pounder thuds down,
a muffled time-bomb
but the ground will not open
under my feet to reveal

Hades and that lost daughter
who swallowed a pomegranate seed.
Yet it's that I'm hungry for,
the taste of survival
and Persephone's luck
to have each year divided
between the living and the dead
to halve a sense of loss
as one would share an apple.

SUNFLOWERS

It's not the glow after glow
of row on row of sunflowers
in Southern France that I see
now, not the goldwork, yellow
petals round pincushion hearts
the natural but almost artificial
brightness that Van Gogh made
emblematic, no, I carry in my head
this more potent picture, the way
hundreds of flowers gone dead stand
still facing the sun, their big hearts
rimmed by withered petals looking
like microphones about to broadcast.

TWO CUT SUNFLOWERS

After Van Gogh

Great bristling hearts
packed with stuff
I can't account for
nor itemise, flowerheads
whose last petals curl
to cling on air, the way
a baby's fingers
won't let go
when they first learn to hold,
these blooms are animal –
hedgehogs, or, rather
coiled balls of brush strokes
that prick the eye as if,
cut down, flowers
that turned towards the sun
now face us to test
how we shape up
to perception,
they're huge fringed eyes
that simply will not close –

AQUILEGIAS

On clear April days
these columbines are lamps
lighting the garden

with their red and blue,
their orangegold and rose,
not Tiffany shades

but richer, older,
and let's not call them
granny-caps

as if domestic shapes
define them.
How were they named?

Of course they do not fly
like doves, nor does their form
hint at the power of eagles,

but, in full sunsets,
they are powerful
as windows of a house

that admit the sky,
extending the eye –
its range, its focus.

These petals let light through
like glass, like windows
coloured, stained

as if the garden now
is holy ground,
Chartres cathedral, say,

with its great rose.

⋈ ON AN ISLAND

What do we travel for
if not to push the self out
like a boat
into the open sea
of changing views?

Now a single olive tree
is both vehicle and map
for where we may and may not go
the way, through a hole in bark,
the eye takes in the sea
then picks its way around
layered twisty shapes
to find, if not a route,
a landscape in each knot
that stops the gaze
as mountains do.

CITADEL ON KEFALONIA

If you look hard enough
you almost see, again,
Mycenae's Lion Gate,
the Beehive Tomb,
oleanders still in bloom,
even La Belle Hélène
where 'An Affair Of The Heart'
took place.

Or so I tell myself
near broken walls
whose cyclopean slabs
do not so much recall
a vanished time
as raise the old conundrum
How did they get from there to here?
Those stones? Our stubborn lives?

⍺ "AND THE GULLS ARE THERE"

(from 'In Nunhead Ceremony' by Charlotte Mew)

"And the gulls are there" –
the line runs through my head
as I walk this blustery day
on the Heath, observing
cruelty of beaks and grace of flight.

Turning from a view of trees,
lake, trompe l'oeil bridge,
into the loo of Kenwood House,
I see, in a blur of white
Charlotte Mew and my sister,
both staring at the floor,
at a bottle of disinfectant.

And Charlotte is telling Mavis
that it is too hard to say
what must not be said,
family shame cannot properly
be uttered, 'need'
is a dirty word. My sister
is nodding her head, yes,
they must wash their mouths out
of dirtyspeak. They drink
the Lysol to the dregs.

Gulls bawl for what they want,
wrecking the air with the cry

of throats that sound damaged.
Outside they swoop to catch
bread thrown above the lake.
Is any bird more poised
to take the sky?

And she is here, my gullible sister
to whom I was no use
and I wish the wind would blow
her clear from heart and head.
A burnt-out imagination
cannot give her back her voice
and nothing can keep the dead
from what they did.

∝ VALENTINE

I'm sorry I had to rush away
with no time to ask you why
you were sitting up in bed
bald as a coot, smoking a pipe,
with that grey whippet sprawled
over the duvet. What happened
to your wig? I'm sorry, too,
I broke your heart,
it was not often that Pa
gave you a Valentine's gift.
Glass perched on the edge of a shelf
is an accident waiting to happen.
If you hadn't tinkled your bell
to call me upstairs again
just as I'd rushed all the way down
to answer the phone
the dog would not have gone barking mad
and wrapped himself round my feet
and my hand would not have lunged
to send the heart flying.
As baubles go I hope you'll admit
it was only kitsch,
but I can see why pa bought it.
If I can find a novelty shop
shall I buy you another?
Does it have to be life-size,
or will it do if it's ruby red
and you can see through it?
It may be a while before I come –
I'll keep in touch.

ROSE BAY WILLOW HERB

Earth has no feelings but it has a heart
that pumps the hardest in a rubbish dump,
on railway banks or edge of road,
I think this, seeing Rose Bay grow,

remembering apparent heartlessness
decades ago when a child
on a plot of waste ground saw
her first wild flowers and picked a bunch
for mother who, on the doorstep,
would not let them in –
"They'll make your mother die," she said.

The child I was remains in shock
each June/July when Rose Bay's pink
becomes the pang of mother saying "No"
to my good flowers.

The trick is always to recover
innocence in seeing this or that –
slug tracks silvering a wall,
the emerald body of a fly in sun,
a dirty pigeon's town neck smudged
with purple, the vividness
of anything even

a mother's silly cry
fraught with colour from life's
underside, as if she'd understood
a foxglove's spotted heart,
and knew the ambivalence of flowers
from folklore long dead and dumb.

But how do I learn to love again
weeds tough enough to break
through hard ground, wayward,
the way forgiveness is
when it finds a crack ?

DOPPELGÄNGER

A boy not seen for decades
comes through a door,
a double-take, my cousin's son
wearing my cousin's face of then
as if a face is merely a hook
for looks to hang onto
when parents pass on
a family expression!

Childless I'll not transmit
even the ghost of a smile
though ghosts obsess me.
One takes me by surprise
down my cousin's hallway
where my mother holds my gaze.
Growing older, I'm stricken
by the force of 'my'.
I look into an unfamiliar mirror

wondering what does it mean
to own a self or body?
Suppose that anxious look of hers
stops here with me? It is not
Clytaemnestra's death-mask,
there's nothing epic
in small domestic tragedies that happen
when mothers become ghosts
while still alive,
and haunt, when dead,
their daughters' eyes.

HENRY MOORE AT KEW

Face sliced off, a woman
cradles a cub or pup,
head formed like a snout –
of course it's a human child
and that exchange of looks
where no eyes and no lips are
retrieve a tenderness
we knew or crave:
look around
have you not seen boulders
hunker down and shape
into what we recognise
as mothers, with or without
a creature in their arms?

Here they stand,
two or three metres high,
stone or moulded bronze,
while women who lie down
on their own turn heads away
from what they won't confront
and gaze toward a there that's
inexact. Nearby, connected
shapes recline, a man
and his own soul, perhaps,
that iron twist inside
a body-cage, the soul
or angel that he wrestles with
or else the twin who died at birth –
did not one die in all of us
who feel the twinge of phantom limbs?

And seeing fat slabs
interlock like Rubik's cubes
I try to work out
what fits where – is anyone
how he/she thinks they look
inside? Our breasts
do not hang right
our legs are splayed,
knees humped and thick
as tree-trunks wait
and this is the weight we bear,
this longing to be larger
than our lives
or, if not that, to be
most powerfully ourselves
when split, divided, broken up.

2.

Near the Orangery
Moore's 'Two Ovals'
are poised on grass,
two huge holes aslant, aligned
to mirror each other's emptiness,
anchored by a subterranean device
fixed to their metal rims.
I walk away, pace back
and suddenly, from a place
suiting my height and size,
see these gaps unite
as one solid form
and I'm riveted, as if the eye
requires only a trick of light,
the play of space and mass,

an artist's sleight of hand,
to glimpse how emptiness
may be transformed
into an archaic goddess who,
lost and damaged, is now found.

EPITHALMIUM IN FEBRUARY

For Avi Spier and Ingrid van Welie

"Pearls of Ice" – Helmittu,
Finns called this month seeing
snowmelt on trees frozen into
gems. February,
the Romans' month of expiation
here atones for winter's depredation
with woods that hold their breath
in unopened buds, teardrop-shaped,
like the pearl worn by the turbaned girl
in Vermeer's painting. Snowdrops
open into bells that quietly tell
the marriage of two seasons,
and, like your wedding, signal hope.

"Pearls of Ice", the phrase
hangs in the mind
an image of gleam and shine
outliving frost, outlasting water-drops,
now here, now gone.
There is an energy in words
that sometimes, like the sun,
makes things change or grow,
for all we know,
the whole world is a metaphor.
At any rate, let's say
the world's your oyster
now you enter into marriage.
Or, to put it in another way,

you become the world's bivalve, containing
grit enough to create
rare brilliancies, children, perhaps,
ideas, inventions, knowledge.
Two people matched in heart and mind
bring, in these dark times,
the pearl of courage.

BLUE ⚔

Sapphire, cobalt, amethyst,
you may list the names
of shades of blue, though
words are poor ghosts
of colour's substance,
ultramarine, say, or indigo
that going into itself
which sea does in a mood
of violet/violent blue
like the purply blue
of sea-holly in the garden
which this year stopped me dead,
thinking, if I looked hard enough
I'd know what it is
to exist intensely
not closed in
by walls, trees, fence –
a blue so immense
there were no limits
to what it might do
flooding the eye
as if it meant
to enter one's lifeblood
like the ocean without horizon
that flowed through a single plant.

RED, MAGENTA GOLD

After the painting *The Gopis Search for Krishna*, Jodhpur, 1765

If there's a beguiling flute
to be heard, these cowherds
feel it with their eyes, note
their aquiline faces
and that sharp attention.
Not that there's music
to begin with. First
there's a house composed
of windows like an Advent
Calendar all opened up.
These 'Gopis' are miracles
of depiction. One rises
golden from her bed
another bathes or bakes,
outside Krishna makes music
while one tiny girl
hennas the soles of her feet.

Souls quiver in this trilogy
of paintings, or maybe I mean
selves which, a philosopher said,
are not found anywhere
embodied, rather they are
a style-of-being-in-the world.
But what's the style-of-being-cowherds-
in-search-of-Krishna to do
with atheist, Catholic, Jew
in Western Europe?

Yet we're here in a museum,
at least, here I am, taken
out of myself, the eye
moved up and down
from left to right, loses itself
in the red, magenta, gold
of headscarves and saris
and the embroidered green of leaves
to find a new perspective

where blue as a monsoon cloud
Krishna clones himself
over and over to appear
to each searching girl the way
blue assumes its heavenly form
for every individual eye,
or so I think, moving
to a new idea of colour
as music, seeing the gopis
wrapped round a rhythm
of trees and not changing
into a tree, like mythic Daphne,
but being at one
with forest and grove –
and that is the difference
between rape and rapture,
that finding a soul-mate.

And we are ravished,
not by Hindu gods
but by the maharaja's painters who
open a house of windows
inside, a space to glimpse,
if only for an instant,
one's own lit soul
among the many glowing details.

SPECTRES

It is archaic now to talk
about the underworld,
how Aeneas recognised
Anchises, though spectres
lacked lips and hands.
We know the dead
are bodiless,
that they're in
an accordion tune
that floats from a window;
they're a phase of weather,
sudden hail or mist
over the hills;
they are inside us
as if there's a space
between bones or in the walls of cells,
that place where we feel
a pang.
They are a change of mood,
as when you're on a beach,
the sun is clear, the sea is calm
and food and wine go down
like the treat they are,
but there is this sudden
desolation.
You don't say a thing, merely wait
till you're returned to where you are
for the leisurely walk back
to where the holiday lives
in someone else's room,
in someone else's sheets
where you lie down.

ANYONE OUT THERE?

Don't you sometimes feel
deep space
looking at you,
deep space empty
as the eyes of a skull?
Doesn't a skull's gaze
go right through you
more than living eyes,
except for lovelight?
Where does that come from
if not the depth behind
the substance of the eye,
from where, at times,
looks take off
like a long-distance plane
that zooms
from sunset to sunset
as if there is no end
to blazing skies?
There is an end to sun and stars,
haven't you seen the eyes
of unrequited lovers
when something dies in them?
Fuck the Big Bang,
the way that galaxies
zero through light years
at the rate of nots –
not here, not there, not anywhere
and then deep space
empty unless it holds
a particle unrealised.
Have you not felt yourself

hugely unseen
by the gaze of that dead God
whom we still talk about,
those lightless eyes behind
deep time, deep space?

FULL MOON AND OWLS

In Cefalu they say
"He who hears an owl
knows someone will die."
But that is true without
full moon or hooting –
the question's always "Who?"
We are at sea investigating
night's apparent sadness.

Yet listening hard one finds
no precise mood in that cry
not grief, fear, confusion,
nothing eerie. It is a sound
that makes space intimate
without a near or far,
only a pale circle where
day's screams and wailing
come to be absorbed
in ululation
shaped like full moon
as if at the heart of night
there is a lighthouse.

MAGPIE ON SNOW

The image won't let go –
perched on a black branch risen
with new white a magpie,
belly and breast less white
than snow, strikes a note
on white's variations, white
that enigma of reflection –

For months I've remembered
bright striations and loaves of snow
on walls and trees, whiter than flour
or those sugar cubes grandpa took
on his tongue or those I dipped
in lemon tea to lose themselves
in orange glow, as sun does in sea.
A blur's behind eyes that have strained
to see a sunset through to its disappearance.

But I want to be clear
about that one bird in one tree,
a woodcut in 3D, an ideogram,
a text spelling out in black and white
how contrasts of light and dark
stand out and astonish
as much as that dazzling flurry
of facts read in childhood
when photographs revealed
snow's inner life –
"No two snowflakes are alike."

If this is also true of people
perhaps a time-lapse movie
one day will show
within or beyond cells and brain
selves uniquely crystalline
to register sensation,
that patterning, say,
of magpie on snow.

WOOD PIGEONS

Those fucking pigeons
deserve clean lines
to articulate
a courteous mating.
Six times the male
bobs his head (tail
quite still) so how
could one not see a bow
of homage and pleading?
And mutual feeding,
is it, when two beaks
open to a meeting
too pecky to be called
French kissing? Then bald
consummation, breast on back
in a balancing act
of sex that looks like love
as in Epstein's 'Doves'
where two birds are stuck
together, the male's neck
swollen. His sculpt
is abstract, tactful,
square and curve combine
in hard-edged lines
to give such shape to copulation
that one's imagination
enters a universal egg
almost expecting impregnation.

WHAT A FISHERMAN TOLD ME

Wrestled aboard, the fish,
still in attack-mode, lay
like a firework display, skin
all flicks, sparks, flecks
of changing colours –
cobalt, turquoise, green
lit up the deck,
sail-fin flashed
ruby-red and madder.
He had not seen before
in dying flesh
light swoop and dazzle
and wondered if he'd caught
a Perseid shower,
Aurora Borealis
or the stuff of original stars
elementally lodged in bodies.
He'd fought the six-foot sail-fish
half an hour, later
he'd lost his appetite
for the dish to follow –
how could he eat stars?

THE STEPS OF HORSES

I'd not expected llamas
on a day like any other,
when I was walking through a field,
grass green as always,
hills the same distance away,
nor had I expected to see
that skewbald pony
with brown patches over his eyes
matched in size and form
as if he'd never need blinkers
and could look wherever he chose.
Six irregular shapes
of brown shag, bulky
with picnic panniers, beside
two men, two women, two boys,
crossed a bridge into the field.
Six periscopic necks
swivelled inquiring eyes
and though cloven feet padded along
soft as bedroom slippers
the pony lifted his hooves and ran.
I hadn't expected to see
something meant to show
what movement is, animal,
but spiritual too – I caught
that morning morning's aerial
happening, a creature on the ground
uplifting itself and swerving
into the wind as if
the steps of horses
at last had found their feet.

HÔTEL ST. RÉMY

After Van Gogh

That block of yellow
where the eye may dwell
is solid building driven
into colour, the eye
zooms into life with pines
that outreach their grasp
of blue. Sun and chemical
have put together a green
they'd have wanted
if they had minds –
a dazzling aspiration
is that what madness is?

We who've been there,
not St. Rémy exactly,
but that sort of place
may recognise a mood
of sanity, of love, when sky
burns through stone
and leaves make light
of what and where they are,
letting go of a green
that's unconfined, letting go
of their hold on trees,
the way we stop
holding on to the wall
of a ward, walking free
into a world that's safe
as houses, solid
as yellow that builds up
into asylum.

TOWARDS A SELF-PORTRAIT

Going under the knife
my flesh will not amaze
like a red-beaded fig's
nor will there be that rush
of red seen in a church
now an Umbrian cave,
pitch-black till one struck match
revealed the flare of saints
on frescoed walls, a gift
of unexpected presence.

For all I know my blood's
a manifold, like Plath's
whose cut thumb sent guardsmen
running. I harbour no
homunculi, surgeons
will only find the stuff
that is red's paradigm,
hue needed, Cézanne said,
for artists' temperament.
If I could paint I'd make

pictures of figs, perhaps,
testicular, each seed
a saint, or else, a church
built into rock become
a womb-like cave that's filled
with medlars, quinces, pears,
and berried, globose fruit,
then my own interior,
vena cava, arteries
by which the heart communicates.

BEFORE THE STORM

The sea is black, coal
or crow, no, not feathery,
an almost lapidary black
as if the sea's achieved
the colour it worked for
shifting through silks and mica,
textures too various to show
its real face. I watch
from the top of a hill
cloud bellying down
and an expanding darkness.

Then, close to, the sea
lets go of itself a little
and there is this first-time blue,
like first snow, too deep
to say, and although
I want to share this new
colour the way we share
the sea, saying "aquamarine"
and "cobalt" and all the shades
between azure and indigo,
I cannot name the hue
black smoulders into
but must take it to myself,
an apperception, private,
as my own death will be.

VENICE, THIS TIME

Now I know what a thunderbolt is,
for, this time in Venice
in the mother of all storms
we returned from San Giorgio
to a vaporetto stop
where a thunder-clap
rumbled a shed's
tin roof, and our heads
ducked as the sky
exploded. A girl ran by
laughing, as if that bang created
a mood of exaltation.

And now I know what it is to be struck
almost dead with fear, thunderstruck
at the row we had, senseless
as the turbulence
of a wasted afternoon,
no you and in bright sun
I couldn't see the city any more
than in the first downpour
that disappeared the canals.
The mind needs rituals
to channel its flood
of disquietude,

a convention like that rainbow
beyond the high window
of our hotel, two days after
the real storm. I hope to remember
its trajectory
over the Salute and Redentore,

a perfect bridge in the sky,
the kind angels, they say,
walk over weeping
into our eyes for all our making
and unmaking of weather
in Venice, or wherever.

MIRRORS

A life can be haunted by what it never was
If that were merely glimpsed...
          —Louis MacNeice

A life can be haunted by what it never was,
but suppose, after all, we were
what we wanted, like Narcissus
who caught sight of himself in a pool.
A life can be haunted by those
we obsessively loved, a lovelife that never was
although we thought we saw lovelight, or felt
a kiss on the back of the neck before
a head could be turned.

Dare we imagine we were what we wanted
wanted and beautiful like that face under water
glimpsed by Narcissus who
could not break through to himself?
A life can be haunted by broken mirrors
distorting our faces
but looking elsewhere we catch sight
of doubles, twins, soul-mates promising
to repair a shattered image –

were they not imprisoned in water.

THE MAN IN FANCY DRESS &

I came to her bed
wearing blue brocade,
a smoking jacket bursting apart
over a quiver of arrows;
I carried my heart in my hands,
unpinned from my sleeve,
but, bored, as always,
she pushed me away.

I came in as a clown,
white Pierrot hat,
black pointy shoes,
stiletto heels, click-clack,
a buffoon of a lover
in baggy pantaloons
making signs with my hands,
when she threw me out,
as if measuring a fish
that had got away.

Changing I wore
a poet's fedora, a red,
silk shirt, recited
Marvell, Donne, Auden
all rolled into a honeyball
of language, irresistible, I thought,
but she pursed her lips to ask
"What do you want from me?"

Then I burned to bits
costumes of hope and desire
and shed, don't ask me how,

flesh and bone and shrank
to nothing at all and stole
into her ear and roared
like an ocean, then flew
onto her tongue like a wasp
blown off course, yet,
lest she bite through me,
entered her brain, a microchip
that made her dream me
weeping, weeping,
because she could not see me.

THE CAVE

(Melissani, Kefalonia)

And it dawned on me in the cave,
seeing snakeheads and limbs
writhe down the walls
and the real dip and skim
of birds near a dome as high
as the water below was deep,
that blue-black lake
on which we were rowed
into this other world,
it came to me, mid-cave,
at the boat's turning point
round a ridge crowded
with bald stumps, stone
rising like fungi
or like shaved balls
that though I'd not seen
the great god Pan,
nor heard his tune,
nor joined his dance,
nor even viewed his statue
found in this 'Cave of Nymphs',
I'd always known a place
built-up by water and stone's
slow copulation
where flesh stiffens into
stalactites that pierce a huge
and overarching darkness.

ON EDGE

Having been on the edge
of something about to happen
had you not stepped back
into a life that meant
to proceed with or without
your consent, you stop
now and then, still
at that moment when
waiting might have become
event, had you not feared
abyss, as if you'd stood
on a window ledge before
police hauled you back,
as if danger and not promise
had been poised on the cusp
of lip and freefall.
What if you'd sloughed the body
that held you in to find
a new skin around you,
new limbs, a lighter head
upheld by broader shoulders?
What if you'd left your life
to go on with or without you,
what then?

'NAKED PORTRAIT' – LUCIAN FREUD ⚯

Every is portrait and everything is autobiographical...

One blind eye peers
from the picture's middle, a hole
between legs crossed, not
to be modest but to show
something as bold as Courbet's
'L'Origine Du Monde', except
this woman has allowed
her shaved vulva to be painted
and there's no pubic fuzz,
no Khalil Bey, only a public
at an exhibition where
this non-eye acquires
a cyclopean focus, compelling
as Mona Lisa's eyes, or
Rembrandt's stare that leads
into depths. Where else
would a gaze want to go
even as it travels up
to a head high on the canvas,
crook'd arm and hand on brow,
then to bedclothes like old snow
under a woman aslant exposing
her openness? Look,
is this a man confronting woman's
absence? I see an aperture
that like a needle's eye
can challenge entry.

WORKING IT OUT

Undead you stood in an expanse
of concrete, a whiteness about you.
Waking, I won't let go of a dream
that could slip away. Was 'concrete'
a visual pun, a hint, dear friend,
we'll never again discuss abstractions –
the real meaning of Freud's dictum
"There's no speech in dreams?"
Where else can we talk with the dead?
Today I'm aware that I said in sleep
"Wherever you are you must find an oasis",
as if on this unbearably bright plain
I missed water and trees.
You held out your hands, palms
upturned, generous as leaves,
asking "What do you want from me
now we're together, at last on firm ground?"

THE DESIRE OF ANGELS

The desire for gold is not gold itself,
but the desire for good is itself good.
—Simone Weil

There's no end to angel fabrication,
gold, bronze, lapis lazuli,
the Annunciation of Fra Angelico
and, if you're disposed to see
how things shape up,
a winter tree holding out two arms
or oil slicks on a road spreading
rainbow-coloured wings.

This Christmas here's a boy who beats
a drum, behind stick-arms wings uplift
as if he's shrugged his shoulders at the world
and had that gesture fixed as extra limbs.
He has thin legs, big feet plonk down
to signify he means to stay.

To signify? Not kitsch,
(he doesn't aspire to art),
he's hardly an iconic angel,
his form does not make visible
a bodiless presence,
he's in your face,
eighteen inches of painted tin.
But, love, we still don't know
how bodies work
now that malignant demons of a kind
have attacked your breast,

so take this reductio ad absurdum of my wish
that you be well guarded –
this boy in boxer shorts and spangly shirt
who beats a drum and looks quite solid.

SECONDS

Time may offer a second chance
or, a chance second, as when
the BBC announced one New Year's Eve

an extra second
would be added on to midnight.
But what was the day supposed to do

with that prolongation –
allow a dying man, perhaps,
one more breath?

From a fast moving car, the other day,
I glimpsed a piebald horse stock-still
in the dullest of winter landscapes.

The roads's here-and-there disappeared
in a second's chance perception
that suddenly gave my breath

the strength to rise and fall
and rise and rise again
to the out-of-time sensation

of a gasp.

STATUES

We'd run flailing our arms
and on a word stopped dead
to hold a pose, a hand
mid-air, a leg askew.

This game came back in Venice:
near the Accademia bridge,
a woman in a headscarf
knelt on stone, head bent.

I'd pass her by at noon,
and towards sunset, vexed
by stillness that commanded eyes
to turn away, or else compelled
a fidgetty attention, small change
dropped in a styrene cup.

Not once did she look up
or shift her legs
under her muslin skirt.

Nobody does that, kneel
for hours on sun-baked ground,
nobody does so much nothing
with their lives as staying still
to earn a livelihood.

And yes, that self-control
gave her a kinship
with fakirs and fire-eaters.

How did she make art
of neediness?

Art? She was in the way
of what I wanted to see,
domes and palace facades.

She shadowed Venice,
and is as large for me
as Colleoni on a horse,

as small as those slippers
by St. Ursula's bed
in Carpaccio's painting,

that emptily wait, askew
(as our own might do)
and steal the picture.

THE UNKNOWN KNIGHT OF NETHERBURY

Look how defaced he is, the way,
lips and nose almost gone, he bears
initials chipped, gouged, carved
onto scabbard and alabaster thighs
by unknown passers-by with knives
that left brow and dog-toothed ruff
intact. Perhaps they did not vandalise
but only left their mark, mere prints,
to last as long as this amputee,
this Sir Anon, who seems to me
lovelier than most statues are,
at least, more real as witness to
the past's attempt at looking noble.
There is the merest hint of paw
where hound and feet should be
to carry a promise through, unbroken.

THE EMPEROR OF EXMOOR

May he rot in hell –
the trophy hunter
who put a stop

to the great stag's rut.
The curse explodes
in my head like

gunshot, not
that I believe in hell
as did St. Hubert

who'd kill
whatever there was to kill
on a bright day in a wood

till that Good Friday when
his dogs pursuing a stag
came to a halt and snarled

and looking up he saw
in tangled antlers
Christ crucified.

Hallucination was it,
sight then sound –
a voice out of the blue

warning damnation?
Or did he really see
something – animal

guilelessness perhaps,
that all too human look
the hunted wear?

Picture the scene
not as medieval monks
confined man and beast

in one lit initial,
nor as tableaux staged
by Breughel or Pisanello

too brightly still, I think,
to realise the action
not in the chase but

in the capture of a vision.
See the caparisoned horse,
and then the nobleman

on his knees on the forest floor
adoring one head in the world
fit to hold God in.